My Gran is a Fibber

Written by Swapna Haddow

Illustrated by Parwinder Singh

Collins

1 Meet my gran

My gran is a fibber.

She is visiting my school to help out.
"Do not tell fibs, Gran," I insist.

"I never fib!" Gran grins.

4

Then Gran tells Tim that there was a shark in our shower.

"Jai, your gran is a fibber," Tim snorts.

Gran tells Sora that she can jump as far as the moon.

"What a fibber!" Sora sniggers.

Gran tells Flora that she once went to the desert and visited the lair of a dragon.

"You are such a fibber!" Flora banters.

9

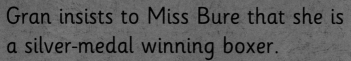

Gran insists to Miss Bure that she is a silver-medal winning boxer.

Miss Bure rubs her chin. "I think that might be a fib —"

2 Gran and her eggs

"Your gran is a fibber!" my pals exclaim.

I slump in my chair. "No! She is just a bit immature!"

13

We row.

I look at Gran. I need her to help me
out now.

"I can gulp down ten eggs in three seconds flat," Gran grins.

I groan.

Gran unzips her handbag.
She pulls out ten eggs.

Gran inserts an egg ...

... and then drops the rest in!

My pals hoot. "Perhaps you are not a fibber."

Gran's grin gets bigger. "Now, let me go and get my dragon!"

Do you think Jai's gran is a fibber?

After reading

Letters and Sounds: Phases 3 and 4

Word count: 217

Focus phonemes: /ch/ /sh/ /th/ /ng/ /ai/ /ee/ /igh/ /oa/ /oo/ /oo/ /ar/ /or/ /ow/ /air/ /ure/ /er/, and adjacent consonants

Common exception words: of, to, the, no, go, I, pulls, are, my, she, me, be, you, do, out, what, once, school, your, our, was, we, when, there

Curriculum links: PSHE: Relationships

National Curriculum learning objectives: Reading/word reading: apply phonic knowledge and skills as the route to decode words; read accurately by blending sounds in unfamiliar words containing GPCs that have been taught; read other words of more than one syllable that contain taught GPCs; Reading/comprehension (KS2): develop positive attitudes to reading and understanding of what they have read by discussing words and phrases that capture the reader's interest and imagination; understand what they read, in books they can read independently, by checking that the text makes sense to them, discussing their understanding and explaining the meaning of words in context; by drawing inferences such as inferring characters' feelings, thoughts and motives from their actions

Developing fluency

- Take turns to read a page, demonstrating how to use expression.
- Ensure that your child pauses at the ellipses (...) on page 19 and notices how they increase the suspense.

Phonic practice

- Focus on /er/ and /ure/ sounds. Ask your child to find words that contain /er/ and /ure/ on the following pages:

    page 20 (*perhaps, fibber*)   page 13 (*immature*)

- Take turns to find /er/ or /ure/ words on pages 5, 7 and 10. (page 5: *shower, fibber*; page 7: *fibber, sniggers*; page 10: *Bure, silver, boxer*)

Extending vocabulary

- Focus on words that tell us about the way characters speak. Turn to page 9 and point to **banters**. Ask your child what sort of speaking tone Flora is using. (e.g. *jokey*)
- Repeat for: page 5: **snorts** (e.g. *disbelieving*) page 7: **sniggers** (e.g. *laughing*)